UNIVER
TEXAS

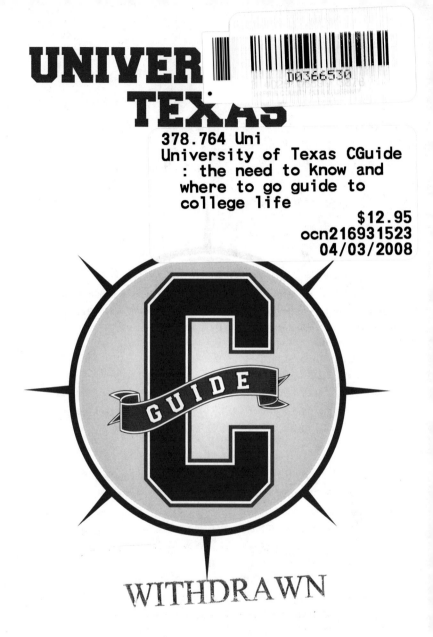

WITHDRAWN

THE NEED TO KNOW AND WHERE TO GO
GUIDE TO COLLEGE LIFE

Published by CGuides Media,
101 Forrest Crossing Boulevard,
Suite 100,
Franklin, TN 37064.

Library of Congress Control Number: 2007908172

CGuides Media is a Waynick Book Group Co.
(615) 277-5555

First Printing, 2008
Printed in the United States
10 9 8 7 6 5 4 3 2 1

Campus Contributor: Jesse A. Gall
Managing Editor: Doan Phuong Hoang Nguyen
Designer: Jay Smith, Juicebox Designs
Production: S.E. Anderson

Visit the CGuides Media Web site at www.cguides.net

http://utexas.cguides.net

UNIVERSITY OF TEXAS

THE NEED TO KNOW AND WHERE TO GO GUIDE TO COLLEGE LIFE

You've had an entire year to prepare for college. Now that you're finally here, you might feel somewhat overwhelmed. Your parents aren't here to take care of you, so you're on your own. You probably have a million questions to ask about life in Austin. Like where's the closest laundromat? What about the best places to eat on campus? And what are the hot spots in town? Well, this *CGuide* is here to help you! Everything you want to know about the University of Texas at Austin can be found in this book. By the end of it, you'll know all about the city and the university.

Don't forget to stay current on UT happenings at the *CGuides* Web site: http://utexas.cguides.net.

TABLE OF CONTENTS

BLAH, BLAH, AND WHATEVER — 102

CAMPUS LIFE
THE BASICS

The University of Texas has a long-established tradition of well-rounded excellence in academia, athletics, and the arts. Founded in 1883, the University of Texas has grown to become one of the largest and most prestigious public schools in the nation. Today the campus encompasses about 350 acres and holds one of the most recognizable buildings in Austin: the Tower. Some 2,200 faculty members work at UT, many of whom also do research. And their talent has not gone unrecognized by the academic community. In the past, various awards—such as the Nobel Prize, the Pulitzer Prize, and the National Medal in Technology—have been awarded to faculty members. With so many talented professors, it's no wonder that in 2007, the University of Texas was ranked 47th in a comprehensive nationwide category and 13th among all public schools.

Not only is UT Austin an amazing school academically, but its athletic department is on fire! For the fourth time in the school's history, UT won the NCAA football national championship at the 2005 Rose Bowl. To this day, the football team continues to be one of the nation's top-ranked teams. UT has won six championships in baseball, two in men's golf, nine in men's swimming, one in women's basketball, one in women's cross country, two in women's tennis, six in women's indoor track and field, five in women's outdoor track and field, and two in volleyball. And that's not to mention the hundreds of Big Twelve Conference championships the Longhorns can brag about.

On top of that, there's always something to do on campus or in the city. Every night, the UT campus is bustling with student activities and events. Don't miss any! Going out into the city is always a fun adventure. Make sure you explore the music scene, the many film festivals, the cultural gatherings, and the riveting nightlife that make Austin so unique.

Your years at UT Austin will be the best years of your life. You'll get all the academic support and life experience you'll need for the "real" world.

VITAL INFO

UNIVERSITY OF TEXAS AT AUSTIN
Austin, TX 78712-1111

MOTTO: "What Starts Here Changes the World"

PRESIDENT: William Powers Jr.

PUBLIC VS. PRIVATE: Public

CAMPUS SIZE: Over 350 acres

MASCOT: Bevo the Longhorn

COLORS: Burnt Orange and White

WEB SITE: www.utexas.edu

STUDENT BODY MAKEUP

There are over 34,000 undergraduate students and 12,000 graduate students enrolled at the University of Texas in the various schools and colleges.

UNDERGRADUATE STUDENTS
16,597 are men
18,265 are women

GRADUATE STUDENTS
6,335 are men
5,761 are women

MAJORS OFFERED

The University of Texas has just about everything you need academically. If you feel like studying Sanskrit or Russian Studies, you can. With one of the largest faculties in America, it's no surprise that UT offers a wide array of majors to fit your interests.

"The diverse options of majors at UT allow you to find your true path and follow it successfully."

– DONALD, Graduate 2007

MINORS OFFERED

Specific minors are allowed in various colleges. Not all colleges have minors though. Some will say you have a "concentration in X" (where X is eighteen hours or more in a given area). Contact your college's advisor to find out specific policies.

To find out more about academics at UT Austin, go to www.utexas.edu/academic.

COLLEGES WITHIN THE UNIVERSITY

SCHOOL OF ARCHITECTURE
This comprehensive school offers two majors that will prepare you for careers in the field of architecture.
http://soa.utexas.edu

MCCOMBS SCHOOL OF BUSINESS
One of the nation's most prestigious business schools, the McCombs School of Business supplies students with comprehensive career paths and state-of-the-art facilities. Four majors are offered.
www.mccombs.utexas.edu

COLLEGE OF COMMUNICATION
One of Texas's most esteemed colleges, the College of Communication is known for its journalism, advertising, public relations, and communication studies paths. There are six majors.
http://communication.utexas.edu

COLLEGE OF EDUCATION
Dedicated to teaching future educators, this college is ranked 8th among public institutions in the nation. The school offers five majors.
www.edb.utexas.edu/education

COLLEGE OF ENGINEERING

This college fosters a learning environment aimed toward helping students develop into the engineers of tomorrow. Students can choose from seven majors.

www.engr.utexas.edu

COLLEGE OF FINE ARTS

From classical dance classes to playwriting, the College of Fine Arts offers some of the best electives any student can take (and even better classes for students enrolled in the college). Eight majors are offered.

www.finearts.utexas.edu

JACKSON SCHOOL OF GEOSCIENCES

Boasting an incredible ability to get prospective students immediately involved in their chosen career path after graduation, it is no wonder that this school consistently ranks within the top ten. Plus, considering that nearly two-thirds of the country's geologists live in Houston, proximity is a good thing! The school offers four majors.

www.jsg.utexas.edu

SCHOOL OF INFORMATION

You may be wondering, *What in the world is a school of information?* Students who attend the school will tell you that it's the nation's number one program in Archives and Preservation. They deal with information, and they do it well. This school only offers a minor to undergraduates.

www.ischool.utexas.edu

SCHOOL OF LAW

One of the nation's oldest law schools, this graduate school is pretty exceptional and offers dual degree programs with the other grad schools at UT.

www.utexas.edu/law

COLLEGE OF LIBERAL ARTS

This college has multiple offerings for major paths, everything from Sanskrit and the Humanities to African-American Studies. Fifty-one majors are offered.

www.utexas.edu/cola

COLLEGE OF NATURAL SCIENCES

The second-largest college at UT, this college is not just your run-of-the-mill science school. It offers science enthusiasts much more! Nine bachelor of arts degrees and forty-six bachelor of science degrees are offered here.
http://cns.utexas.edu

SCHOOL OF NURSING

One of the best nursing programs in the state of Texas, this school is nationally ranked as one of the top twenty master's programs in the nation. If being a nurse seems to be in your future, then becoming a Longhorn is too. Only one major is offered.
www.utexas.edu/nursing

COLLEGE OF PHARMACY

This college contains some of the best facilities offered to students, along with access to hands-on experience at the Student Health Services pharmacy. This college only offers one major.
www.utexas.edu/pharmacy

LBJ SCHOOL OF PUBLIC AFFAIRS

Preparing students to address the world's most important public policy problems, this graduate school is not only important, it's prestigious.
www.utexas.edu/lbj

SCHOOL OF SOCIAL WORK

The undergraduate program combines liberal arts with social work classes to provide a wider basis of expertise that students can take into the workforce. Only one major is offered.
www.utexas.edu/ssw

ATHLETICS

The University of Texas has one of the best athletic scenes in the nation, and you can't avoid it (even if you want to)! You might as well embrace the fun. Texas sports are everywhere, so go ahead and buy your orange sweater now!

CONFERENCE
Big Twelve

MASCOT
Bevo the Longhorn

COLORS
Burnt Orange and White

MEN'S SPORTS
Football
Baseball
Basketball
Golf
Swimming and Diving
Tennis
Track and Field/
Cross-country

WOMEN'S SPORTS
Basketball
Golf
Rowing
Soccer
Softball
Swimming and Diving
Tennis
Track and Field/
Cross-country
Volleyball

"There are very few things as fun as walking into a packed stadium right before a game. It's electric."

— RINA, Senior

FIGHT SONG

Texas Fight! Texas Fight!
    And it's good-bye to A&M.
Texas Fight! Texas Fight!
    And we'll put over one more win.
Texas Fight! Texas Fight!
    For it's Texas that we love best.
Hail, Hail, the gang's all here,
    And it's good-bye to all the rest!
Yea, Orange! Yea, White!
    Yea, Longhorns! Fight! Fight! Fight!
Texas Fight! Texas Fight!
    Yea, Texas Fight!
Texas Fight! Texas Fight!
    Yea, Texas Fight!
The "Eyes of Texas" are upon you,
        All the live long day!
           The "Eyes of Texas"
           are upon you,
        You cannot get away!
        Texas Fight!
        Texas Fight!
        For it's Texas
          that we love best!
      Hail, Hail,
        the gang's all here!
And it's good-bye to all the rest!

CAMPUS HOUSING

By the time you enter your freshmen year, you've probably been inundated with horror stories about freshmen housing. But not to worry, there isn't a single dorm at the University of Texas at Austin that doesn't have at least one great thing about it. And unlike other universities, UT doesn't require its students to live in the dorms. Dorms are given away on a first-come, first-served basis. So if you want to live off campus, you can.

THE DORMS

- Most of the dorms are coed, with the exception of **Kinsolving** (women's), **Littlefield** (women's), and **Simkins** (men's). Both **Littlefield** and **Simkins** have community bathrooms and moveable furniture. **Littlefield** has verandas, several study rooms, and sinks in most rooms. **Simkins** has the advantage with a kitchenette, sand volleyball courts, and barbeque pits. The women in **Kinsolving** have rooms with connecting bathrooms, limited community bathrooms, in-dorm dining, a patio, a computer lab, a sun deck, and a piano.

- **Andrew**, **Blanton**, and **Carothers** are coed dorms cropped together to form the Honors Quad. They share the Honors Quad Courtyard and have community baths. Both **Blanton** and **Carothers** have sundecks; **Carothers** has a computer lab.

- If you enjoy working out, check out **Duren** and **Jester.** Located next to the gym and library, **Jester** has in-dorm dining, private connecting or community baths (depending on the room), study rooms on each floor, and a TV room. **Duren** has a game and exercise room, a private courtyard, a lounge on each floor, and video surveillance on exterior doors and elevator lobbies.

- **Brackenridge** is connected to **Roberts**. Both have community baths, movable bunk beds, TV rooms, and study lounges.

- **Prather** and **Moore-Hill** both have laundry facilities, community bathrooms, and moveable bunk beds. Moore-Hill has a recreation room.

- **San Jacinto** has an in-dorm convenience store, a computer lab, an amphitheater, study rooms, and lounges on every floor.

- **Whitis Court** has community bathrooms and kitchens, living rooms, and is near the Drag.

TIP

Take the time to browse the virtual tours of the rooms and living spaces at the housing Web site before you decide on a place to live. And think about whether a coed dorm or a same-sex dorm would better suit your desired freshmen year experience. www.utexas.edu/student/ housing

● CAMPUS DINING

The University of Texas offers a wide array of on-campus dining so you'll never get bored with your daily meals. You'll always have the option to try something different and affordable. A quick tip: Switching around your "usual" meal will keep you from getting sick of dorm food too quickly. And don't burn out on Ramen Noodles either!

- **CYPRESS BEND**
  309 E. 21st St.

- **JESTER CITY LIMITS**
  309 E. 21st St.

- **JESTER CITY MARKET**
  201 E. 21st St.

- **JESTER SECOND FLOOR DINING ROOM**
  201 E. 21st St.

- **KINSOLVING**
  2605 Whitis Ave.

- **KINS MARKET**
  2605 Whitis Ave.

- **LITTLEFIELD PATIO CAFÉ**
  2503 Whitis Ave.

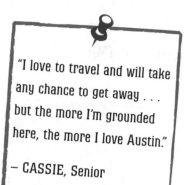

"I love to travel and will take any chance to get away . . . but the more I'm grounded here, the more I love Austin."

— CASSIE, Senior

◉ NOTES

_____

_____

_____

_____

_____

_____

_____

_____

_____

_____

_____

_____

_____

_____

NUMBERS TO HAVE ON SPEED DIAL

Athletic Events: **(512) 471-4602**

Housing and Food Service: **(512) 471-6021**

Frank C. Erwin Jr. Special Events
Center: **(512) 477-6060**

② CAMPUS LIFE
THE DETAILS

The University of Texas at Austin has a vibrant and energetic campus. With over nine hundred registered organizations on campus, students always have something to do. And if you want to get involved, there are so many ways you can. If you want to enhance your academic experience outside of the classroom, join an academic club. And for those who enjoy playing sports, then consider playing intramural or club sports. Both are great ways to make friends while staying in shape. If that doesn't interest you, what about Greek life?

GREEK LIFE

Greek life is the backbone of social interactions at many universities, but here at the University of Texas, that's not the case. Eleven percent of the student population is Greek and 89 percent is not. But don't be worried about the small number because 11 percent of nearly forty thousand students is still a pretty large social network. Nearly four thousand students participate in the Greek system, so if you want to immerse yourself in the Greek life, your options are almost endless. But if you want to avoid the Greeks, the large size of the school allows you to do just that. There are currently over fifty different Greek chapters at the University of Texas.

CLUBS AND ORGANIZATIONS

The University of Texas offers a selection of student organizations that's just as diverse as the student body. You can have your pick from more than nine hundred registered student organizations on campus. From the Anime Club to the Law School's musical group Assault and Flattery, there is something for everyone.

POLITICAL ORGANIZATIONS

If you're interested in politics, then get started early and join any of the student political organizations. You can find all types of groups—from Students for a Democratic Society to the International Socialist Movement.

"I love my sorority. I had a place to stay, with girls I loved hanging out with, and I met a lot of new people."

– ASHLEY, Senior

SOCIAL ORGANIZATIONS

UT Austin has a variety of social organizations outside the Greek system. From the Mac Users Group to the Longhorn Hellraisers, there is definitely something for everyone.

RELIGIOUS ORGANIZATIONS

For those of you who want to participate in religious organizations, you have many options. There are various Buddhist, Islamic, Jewish, and Christian organizations available.

For more information on student organizations available, go to http://deanofstudents.utexas.edu/sald/studentorgs/index.php.

INTRAMURALS

if you're looking for an organization that's in the realm of physical activity, then intramural sports are a great option. The classics of basketball and flag football are offered, along with the unique ones like water volleyball, handball, and sports trivia bowl. Create your own team or join a tournament for an individual sport at any skill level. To find out more about intramurals and how to join, visit www.utrecsports.org/intramurals/about.php.

CLUB SPORTS

If intramural sports aren't your bag, then maybe club sports are. A wide variety of club sports are available, from fencing to archery to basketball. There are forty-three sports in total. It's a fun way to make friends while playing your favorite sport. To find out more about club sports and how to join, visit www.utrecsports.org/sportclubs.

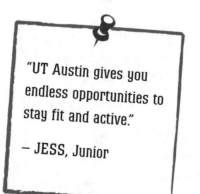

"UT Austin gives you endless opportunities to stay fit and active."

– JESS, Junior

CONFERENCE ATHLETICS

There's electricity in the air. You see blazes of orange and white everywhere. You sit down in your seat, not knowing that the energy of the stadium will force you to your feet in a matter of minutes. The students around you will start singing "Give 'em Hell," and screaming ensues. You will join them, even though you know your vocal chords will hurt the next day. But it's all worth it because you've witnessed the best game ever! And this is just a typical day in UT athletics.

Longhorn students are probably the most passionate fans in the country, and they have plenty of reason to be. With national championships in football, baseball, men's golf, men's and women's swimming and diving, volleyball, women's basketball, women's cross-country, women's track and field, and women's tennis, it's no wonder that sports are HUGE here. UT, one of the top-rated athletic programs across the board, is constantly being matched up with some of the greatest opposing teams across the country. It's no wonder UT's games are so much fun.

But UT athletics is more than just watching sports. It's a part of the college experience and being a Longhorn. And if it's a big win, the fun doesn't stop at the game. The tower is doused in orange, and on the drag, every car will honk their horns mercilessly, creating mass pandemonium and a sense of relentless joy.

You'll never have as much fun as you will at UT games. Join in the fun, even if it means getting doused with orange and white paint!

HOW TO SECURE TICKETS
Now, this part can be a little tricky since each sport has its own rules on how to get tickets. However, one thing is constant: buy the Longhorn Sports Package. It is $80, and you get tickets to every athletic event on campus.

Getting football tickets is a little different. Because it's the most popular sporting event on campus, tickets are given away in a lottery. About a week before the game, every student will have a few days to go pick up a bracelet with a number on it, and if your number is called, you get a ticket. It sounds bad, but they release about three thousand numbers for every game, so many students can get a ticket.

Basketball is a little simpler. To sit in the student section, you simply have to get in line and hope that they don't run out of tickets.

Ticket Box Office: (800) 982-BEVO
Ticket Box Office Two: (512) 471-3333

TIP

When you need to find out exactly when certain sporting events are happening, the best and easiest way is to pick up The Daily Texan, the student newspaper. It has a sports section, and one section is dedicated to upcoming sporting events.

LIBRARIES

There are more than enough libraries for any student at UT to riffle through. Some students think that there are a few too many. So, in an effort to make it a little easier, let's break it down to the few libraries you need to know about.

PERRY-CASTANEDA LIBRARY (PCL)

Located across the street from Jester dormitory, this is the mother of all libraries. The PCL has six floors of literature and houses one of the largest computer labs on campus. This will be the place where most of your studying occurs. Not only that, but most of the books you will need are at this giant of a library.

> 101 East 21st St.
> (S.W. corner of Speedway and 21st)
> **Phone: (512) 495-4300**
> **Hours vary per semester**

UNDERGRADUATE LIBRARY (UGL) / THE FLAWN ACADEMIC CENTER (FAC)

What used to be a library with actual books has now become a four-story building to study in. Complete with oversized beanbags, couches, and plenty of table space, this "library" is one of the best places to study indoors on the campus. But don't think the UGL doesn't have something more to offer. The Audio-Visual Library located inside the UGL should not go underappreciated. It offers a recent and comprehensive DVD library that students can rent from like at Blockbuster, but it's free!

> Located right next to the Student Union
> **Phone: (512) 495-4440**
> **Hours vary per semester**

FINE ARTS LIBRARY

The Fine Arts Library is a great place, if you happen to be interested in keeping up with your play reading or just need to check out that play that your fine arts teacher is making you read. It's a fun library with some very interesting literature.

> Located on the third floor of the Doty Fine Arts Building
> **Phone: (512) 495-4480**
> **Hours vary per semester**

COMPUTER LABS

Computer labs are available in various buildings on campus. Some are open to all UT students, faculty, and staff while others are more restricted.

FOR GENERAL USE (all UT faculty, staff, and students)

- GRADUATE SCHOOL OF BUSINESS BUILDING
- PERRY-CASTANEDA LIBRARY (PCL)
- ERNEST COCKRELL JR. HALL (ECJ)
- PETER T. FLAWN ACADEMIC CENTER (FAC)
- MULTIMEDIA COMPUTER FACILITY (MCF)
- ROBERT LEE MOORE HALL (RLM)

SHARED USE (you must have an ITS account with PRS service)

- EXPERIMENTAL SCIENCE BUILDING (ESB)
- ROBERT A. WELCH HALL (WEL)

RESTRICTED USE (you must be a student in a specific school/major)

- W. R. WOOLRICH LABORATORIES (WRW)
- SUTTON HALL (SUT)
- ART BUILDING AND MUSEUM (ART)
- CHEMICAL AND PETROLEUM ENGINEERING BUILDING (CPE)
- PHARMACY BUILDING (PHR)
- T. S. PAINTER HALL (PAI)
- PARLIN HALL (PAR)
- GEORGE I. SÁNCHEZ BUILDING (SZB)
- ENGINEERING TEACHING CENTER II (ETC)

- SID RICHARDSON HALL (SRH)

- BURDINE HALL (BUR)

- MEZES HALL (MEZ)

- MCCOMBS SCHOOL OF BUSINESS (CBA)

- SARAH M. AND CHARLES E. SEAY BUILDING (SEA)

- NURSING SCHOOL (NUR)

- F. LOREN WINSHIP DRAMA BUILDING (WIN)

- APPLIED COMPUTATIONAL ENGINEERING AND SCIENCES BUILDING (ACE)

- ROBERT A. WELCH HALL (WEL)

COPY CENTERS

Other than the libraries, the best place to go for on-campus copies is the **Union**. Conveniently located right next to all of the fast food restaurants, the Union has a small little copy center that can meet all of your needs. And if you get there early in the morning, copies are only four cents a piece! If you buy a copy card, you can use it at any of the copy machines in the libraries or copy centers.

"Buy a copy card–it saved me a lot of time and hassle freshmen year."

– JIM, Sophomore

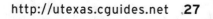

OTHER PLACES TO STUDY

THE BIOLOGY POND OR "THE TURTLE POND"

This is one of the best places to study. It's next to the Union and behind the Tower. It features a multilevel pond with waterfalls and plenty of turtles who just love to climb out of the water during the day. If you come here often, you'll find students trying to cram or artists looking for inspiration.

THE FAC

When it gets too hot outside, just head over to the Flawn Academic Center. They've got the perfect air-conditioned study spot. The FAC features oversized beanbags, sofas, large tables, power outlets for computers, personal desks, and multiple computer labs. It's a great place for meetings or personal study sessions.

THE PCL UPPER FLOORS

If it's a quiet place you seek, then the PCL is the place to be. The upper floors, like the sixth-floor stacks, stay pretty quiet. You can really concentrate on your work here.

THE SIX PACK'S FIELD

There is a large grassy area between two sides of the Six Pack that is great for picnics, hanging out, or reading that last biology chapter. It's lined with giant shady trees and features a great view of the Tower and the fountain that faces 21st Street.

TRANSPORTATION AND PARKING

CAMPUS
DETAILS

Parking on the UT campus is one of the most difficult aspects for freshmen to figure out. Without a permit, parking is almost impossible because the residential areas west and north of campus are pretty much the only options you have. The best way to get a spot is to get there early and park in the first place available.

For a little more insurance, you should get a parking permit. Undergraduates can get C permits, which allows you to park in the designated parking lots right off campus. Buses constantly run from these lots to campus, making it even easier. Plus, you get free parking in restricted spots on weekends and weekday nights. Check out the specifics at the parking Web site: www.utexas.edu/parking.

BUSES

Buses conveniently run on and off campus all day. If the weather gets a little too hot for a fifteen-minute walk to your next class, the Forty Acres bus route will become your best friend. Buses run into the wee hours of the morning. But be careful at night because as it gets later, the buses arrive less frequently.

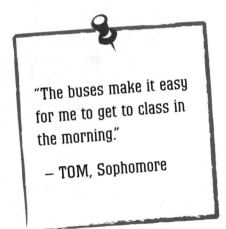

"The buses make it easy for me to get to class in the morning."

– TOM, Sophomore

⦿ SECURITY ON CAMPUS

The University of Texas has its own police department to keep you safe. At orientation, you're told to store the UTPD's phone number in your cell phone, and this is a wise decision. Just call them if you ever need some help.

Another way to reach the UTPD is through the yellow boxes with bright blue lights. Simply hit the red button in them and UTPD will send an officer there within three minutes. If it's a life-threatening emergency, always call 911.

UTPD also offers a security watch e-mail program that you can subscribe to, and they'll send you e-mails about criminal matters on campus.

> Emergency: 911
> Nonemergency: (512) 471-4441

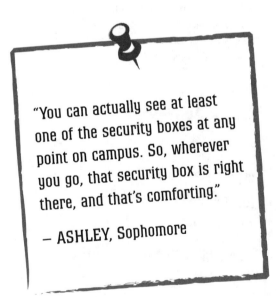

"You can actually see at least one of the security boxes at any point on campus. So, wherever you go, that security box is right there, and that's comforting."

— ASHLEY, Sophomore

TRADITIONAL CAMPUS EVENTS

ACTIVITIES FAIR
During the first few weeks of the school year, organizations set up tables across campus, hoping to increase their enrollment numbers and get students involved early.

ORANGE AND WHITE BALL
Just because you aren't in high school anymore doesn't mean that you can't have fun getting dressed up and going to a pointless formal. The Orange and White Ball occurs at the end of the year, generally in late April or early May, and attracts some beautiful dresses and makes for some even prettier pictures.

GREEK WEEK
Every year the Greek community participates in Greek week, a philanthropic event designed to help raise money for an AIDS research foundation. Festivities include tug-of-war, wing-eating contests, and a 5K run.

CAMPUS DETAILS

"Greek week is the best time of the year! It's so much fun!"

– CASSIE, Senior

GONE TO TEXAS

This event is simply a must for new students! Held every August right before classes start, freshmen gather in the West Mall for live music and welcoming presentations held by each school. This is a good way to have some fun and meet new people.

VOLUNTEER OPPORTUNITIES

Texans are more giving than people think. In fact, the University of Texas is committed to providing students with opportunities to volunteer. Log on to www.utvolunteer.org to search available volunteer possibilities.

THE AUSTIN BATS

Possibly one of the best traditions in Austin is watching the bats swarm out from under their bridge at dusk. People line up to see those bats as if they expect them to fly differently. It's a weird type of fun. August is the best time to see these bats in action because the newborn bats are just starting to hunt with their mothers. They live under the Congress Avenue Bridge over Town Lake.

TIP

Before August ends, take a trip to the Congress Avenue Bridge to see the bats fly out. It's awesome!

◉ NOTES

CAMPUS
DETAILS

NUMBERS TO HAVE ON SPEED DIAL

UTPD: **(512) 471-4441**

Ticket Box Office: **(800) 982-BEVO**

Ticket Box Office Two: **(512) 471-3333**

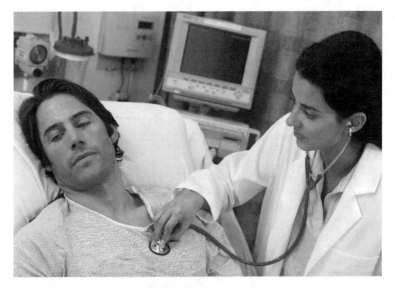

③ TO YOUR HEALTH

Not to be a downer, but taking care of yourself during your time here is crucial to succeeding socially, academically, and most importantly healthwise. It is exceedingly easy to forget to sleep, especially if you're pulling all-nighters every time you have a test. If you can't get enough sleep at night, then nap during the day. Naps are a wonderful thing, and you will learn to love them. Also, don't forget to eat healthy. Try to fit in at least one vegetable in your meals. Eating and sleeping right will help you feel better in class and do better on exams.

◉ CAMPUS HEALTH CLINIC

UT has one of the easiest and most hassle-free health-care systems you could find. The Student Services Building (SSB) houses its own pharmacy and a call-in clinic. Call the Nurse Advice Line and determine if you need an appointment. If you do, the nurse will set it up right there. It's easy and simple: the way things should be when you're sick. Located in the Student Services Building, the Nurse Advice Line is available twenty-four hours a day, and the clinic accepts appointments from eight o'clock in the morning until five o'clock at night, Mondays through Fridays. They're closed on the weekends.

TO YOUR
HEALTH

Nurse Advice Line: (512) 475-6877
University Health Services (UHS): (512) 471-4955
Pharmacy: (512) 471-1824

"If I'm not feeling well, the first thing I do is call the Nurse Advice Line. It's always better safe than sorry."

– CAMERON, Junior

LOCAL HOSPITALS

ST. DAVID'S MEDICAL CENTER
919 E. 32nd St.
Phone: (512) 476-7111

NORTH AUSTIN MEDICAL CENTER
12221 N. Mopac
Phone: (512) 901-1000

SOUTH AUSTIN MEDICAL CENTER
901 W. Ben White Blvd.
Phone: (512) 447-2211

BRACKENRIDGE HOSPITAL
601 E. 15th St.
Phone: (512) 324-7000

TIP

If there's a real medical emergency, head to the hospital ASAP. Don't wait—your health is worth it!

WALK-IN CLINICS/MINOR EMERGENCY CLINICS

PEOPLE'S COMMUNITY CLINIC
2909 N. I-35
Phone: (512) 478-4939
Hours: Monday-Thursday, 8:45 a.m. - 8:30 p.m.
Friday, 8:30 a.m. - 4:30 p.m.
Closed on weekends

AUSTIN REGIONAL CLINIC BRYKER WOODS
3708 Jefferson, Suites 102 and 103
Phone: (512) 452-2244
Hours: Monday-Friday, 8:00 a.m. - 5:00 p.m.

ARC FAR WEST (URGENT CARE)
6835 Austin Center Blvd.
Phone: (512) 346-6611
Hours: Monday-Friday, 7:30 a.m. - 4:30 p.m. and
5:00 p.m. - 9:00 p.m.
Saturday-Sunday, 8:00 a.m. - 5:00 p.m.

WOMEN'S HEALTH

AUSTIN WOMEN'S CLINIC
4101 James Casey St. #350
Phone: (512) 443-6100
Hours: Monday-Friday (except Wednesday),
9:00 a.m. - 5:30 p.m.
Wednesday, 9:00 a.m. - 2:00 p.m.

CAPITAL OBSTETRICS AND GYNECOLOGY
313 E. 12th St. #104
Phone: (512) 324-8670
Hours: Monday-Friday, 8:00 a.m. - 5:00 p.m.

EYE CLINICS

AUSTIN VISION CENTER
2415 Exposition Blvd. #D
Phone: (512) 477-2282
Hours: Monday–Friday, 9:00 a.m. - 6:00 p.m.

ECLECTIC EYEWEAR
2510 Guadalupe St.
Phone: (512) 472-4498
Hours: Monday–Friday, 9:30 a.m. - 6:00 p.m.
        Saturday, 9:30 a.m. - 5:00 p.m.

STUDENT COUNSELING SERVICES

Sometimes adjusting to college and classes can be emotionally draining. If you need someone to talk to or just have some questions, stop by the SSB for free answers and counseling services. At UT Austin, counseling comes in many forms: one-on-one sessions with therapists, help lines, online tips to relax, group therapy, and even an online assessment test to diagnose eating and drinking problems. UT psychiatrists are available to diagnose problems and help students in any way they can.
www.utexas.edu/student/cmhc

UT COUNSELING AND MENTAL HEALTH CENTER
SSB 5th Floor
Phone: (512) 471-3515
Hours: Monday–Friday, 8:00 a.m. - 5:00 p.m.

NOTES

NUMBERS TO HAVE ON SPEED DIAL

Nurse Advice Line: **(512) 475-6877**

University Health Services
(UHS): **(512) 471-4955**

Counseling/Mental Health: **(512) 471-3515**

④ LOCAL SERVICES
SURVIVING ON YOUR OWN

Now that you're in college, you've got to learn how to survive without your parents. Your mom can't do your laundry anymore (unless she lives in Austin), and luckily for you, there are laundry rooms in many of the dorms. But make sure you bring plenty of quarters for those pesky machines. And don't only do the laundry when ALL your clothes are dirty because you'll be up all night sitting in the laundry room. Laundry won't be your only new responsibility. You've got to manage your finances, take care of your car, and find a dry cleaner all on your own! You can find these places and any other local services you may need in this chapter.

"The Drag (Guadalupe Street) is great! It has a place for dorm decoration, fun eyewear, Texas-inspired cheese steaks, vintage clothing, a university bookstore, and pretty much anything you could need."

– BIMAL, Graduate

◉ BANKS

The UT campus is littered with ATMs and little banks. Bank of America ATMs are located next to the Co-Op, Jamba Juice, the PCL, and the Union. University Credit recently opened a bank right on Guadalupe Street (also known as "The Drag").

BANK OF AMERICA UT–BEVO'S
2304 Guadalupe St.
Austin, TX 78705
Phone: (512) 708-3050
Hours: Monday–Friday, 10:00 a.m. - 4:00 p.m.

BANK ONE UNIVERSITY
1904 Guadalupe St.
Austin, TX 78705
Phone: (512) 236-3070
Hours: Monday–Friday, 9:00 a.m. - 6:00 p.m.
Saturday, 9:00 a.m. - 3:00 p.m.

WASHINGTON MUTUAL
2414 Guadalupe St.
Austin, TX 78705
Phone: (512) 476-8644
Hours: Monday–Friday, 9:00 a.m. - 6:00 p.m.
Saturday, 9:00 a.m. - 1:00 p.m.

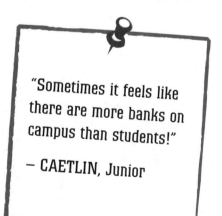

"Sometimes it feels like there are more banks on campus than students!"

– CAETLIN, Junior

DRY CLEANERS

Every now and then you might have a smell that Febreeze just can't get out, so you need to head to the dry cleaners. But without a car, what options do you have? Plenty! The following joints are affordable and will launder, alter, or dry clean your clothing. Not to mention they are just as close as the McDonald's. If you can justify a walk to eat junk food, you should be able to go get your clothes cleaned.

IVORY CLEANERS
1901 Rio Grande St.
Austin, TX 78705
Phone: (512) 472-1730

JACK BROWN CLEANERS
615 W. Martin Luther King Jr. Blvd.
Austin, TX 78701
Phone: (512) 478-4621

UNIVERSITY CLEANERS
2021 Guadalupe St.
Austin, TX 78705
Phone: (512) 469-5635

⊚ HAIR AND NAIL SALONS

ZIG ZAG SALON
3200 Guadalupe St.
Austin, TX 78705
Phone: (512) 467-9774

MANE EXPRESS HAIR SALON
2025 Guadalupe St. Ste. 128
Austin, TX 78705
Phone: (512) 474-4191

FUNNY NAILS SALON AT DOBIE MALL
2025 Guadalupe St., Ste. 124
Austin, TX 78705
Phone: (512) 505-0847

SOPHIA'S BEAUTY AND BARBER SALON
2512 Guadalupe St.
Austin, TX 78705
Phone: (512) 499-0225

RICK'S AVEDA CONCEPT HAIR AND NAIL SALON
2416 Guadalupe St.
Austin, TX 78705
Phone: (512) 476-6960

⊚ FLORISTS AND JEWELERS

CALLA FLORIST AND GIFTS

3701 Guadalupe St.
Austin, TX 78705
Phone: (512) 453-2552

CHARLOTTE'S FIESTA FLOWERS

(voted the best florist in Austin)
3822 N. Lamar Blvd.
Austin, TX 78756
Phone: (512) 453-7619

SHIKI

(Clothing and Jewelry)
3016 Guadalupe #200
Austin, TX 78705
Phone: (512) 371-7767

GALLERIE JEWELERS

3500 Jefferson St., Ste. 105
Austin, TX 78731
Phone: (512) 451-3889

For on-campus jewelry, there's a small outdoor market in between
Jamba Juice and the Co-Op near 24th and Guadalupe.

COMPUTER REPAIR, CELL PHONE SERVICES AND REPAIRS

Have a computer problem? Contact the **ITS Help Desk** at the university or simply walk into the **Campus Computer Store** located in the UGL/FAC. Another option is the local **Geek Squad**.

ITS HELP DESK
Located in the FAC, room 200
Phone: (512) 475-9400

CAMPUS COMPUTER STORE
Located in the FAC
Phone: (512) 475-6550
Hours: Monday–Friday, 8:00 a.m. – 6:00 p.m.

GEEK SQUAD
Phone: (800) 433-5778

AUSTIN CELL PHONE REPAIR
1311 S. Lamar Blvd.
Austin, TX 78704
Phone: (512) 440-8778

POST OFFICES AND SHIPPING SERVICES

UNIVERSITY STATION POST OFFICE
Basement of West Mall Building
Phone: (512) 232-5488

FEDEX SHIP CENTER
327 Congress Ave.
Austin, TX 78701
Phone: (512) 472-4448

CAR SERVICES

JIFFY LUBE SERVICE CENTER
3809 Guadalupe St.
Austin, TX 78751
Phone: (512) 451-3708

H20 HAND CAR WASH
500 S. Lamar Blvd.
Austin, TX 78704
Phone: (512) 236-9274

PLEASANT VALLEY CAR WASH
2500 Willow Hill Dr.
Austin, TX 78741
Phone: (512) 326-4500

GOVERNMENT SERVICES

DMV

6121 N. Lamar Blvd.
Austin, TX 78752
Phone: (512) 936-2100

DMV

1500 N. Congress Ave.
Austin, TX 78704
Phone: (512) 936-2100

DMV

4719 S. Congress Ave.
Austin, TX 78745
Phone: (512) 444-5241

AUTO TITLE SERVICE

2321 E. Cesar Chavez St. #B
Austin, TX 78702
Phone: (512) 472-1557

SOCIAL SECURITY ADMINISTRATION

1029 Camino La Costa
Austin, TX 78752
Phone: (512) 206-3700

TRAVIS COUNTY VOTER REGISTRATION

203 Colorado St.
Austin, TX 78767
Phone: (512) 854-9473

GOING HOME

The **Austin-Bergstrom International Airport** is the closest airport to the UT Austin campus. The fastest way to get to the airport is simply to ask a friend for a ride. But if you can't find anyone, you have several options. You can take a taxi, **SuperShuttle**, or the **Airport Shuttle**.

If you use **SuperShuttle**, their blue and yellow vans will pick you up and take you to your airport terminal. The vans usually come within fifteen minutes of the scheduled pickup time.

SUPERSHUTTLE
Call for Reservations: (512) 258-3826

The **Airport Flyer** is another easy way to get to the airport. It is a shuttle that picks you up from campus and takes you to the airport terminal for a small fee. It's pretty cheap, but the travel time to the airport can be a headache, depending on the number of stops it makes. If you take it, make sure you set aside an extra hour or two before your flight departs. You can buy tickets on their Web site.

AIRPORT FLYER
www.capmetro.org
Phone: (512) 474-1200

If dragging your luggage to the bus stop seems unbearable, then just take a good old-fashioned cab to get to the airport. Usually a trip to the airport from campus will cost you about $20.

AMERICAN YELLOW CHECKER CAB
Phone: (512) 452-9999

AUSTIN CAB
Phone: (512) 478-2222

ROY'S TAXI
Phone: (512) 482-0000

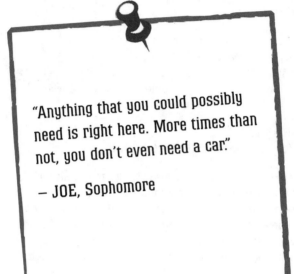

"Anything that you could possibly need is right here. More times than not, you don't even need a car."

— JOE, Sophomore

◉ NOTES

NUMBERS TO HAVE ON SPEED DIAL

Bank of America: **(512) 708-3050**

University Cleaners: **(512) 469-5635**

Zig Zag Salon: **(512) 467-9774**

Charlotte's Fiesta Flowers: **(512) 453-7619**

5 WHERE TO EAT
& WHERE TO MEET

Every college student knows the joy of a good restaurant, a cheap buy, or a great party spot, which is why no one else can be as reliable to let you in on the secrets of the hottest eating spots around campus as college students themselves. From the best date restaurants to the best places to take your parents, you'll find everything in this chapter!

This guide will keep you away from the nasty beasts of food and guide you to the beauties! And you'll find all the regular hotspots to meet new people and make friends.

MEAL PLAN OPTIONS

If you live on campus in the dormitories, your housing contract includes a meal plan that gives you $1,200 **Dine-In Dollars** and $300 **Bevo Bucks**. This allows you to eat twelve meals per week.

Dine-In Dollars are different than **Bevo Bucks** because they can only be used at on-campus dining centers. **Bevo Bucks** can be used both on and off campus. You can also use these bucks in the laundry rooms, computer labs, and vending machines.

If you run out of Dine-In Dollars, you can always add more to your account. You can also transfer Bevo Bucks to become Dine-In Dollars. For more information, go to the Division of Housing and Food Service Web site at www.utexas.edu/student/housing.

WHERE TO EAT

TIP

To add money to your Bevo Bucks account, go to https://utdirect.utexas.edu/bevobuck.

TOP ON-CAMPUS RECOMMENDATIONS

- **CHIPOTLE:** They have the best burritos.

- **MELLOW MUSHROOM:** The cheese bread with marinara is full of flavor and is so good.

- **VEGGIE HEAVEN:** Get the Protein 2000. It's awesome.

- **AUSTIN'S PIZZA:** Order their classic pepperoni pizza; it'll take your breath away.

- **KERBEY LANE CAFE:** The Kerbey Queso is good stuff.

- **SLICES AND ICES:** The garlic knots and cheese pizza are a delicious combination.

- **MADAM MAMS:** The Chicken Pad Thai will leave you wanting more.

OFF-CAMPUS DINING

If you need a break from on-campus food, head to any of the local restaurants in Austin. Whatever you're craving, you can find it in one of the off-campus eateries. You have a variety of choices—everything from Mexican to Italian. Some restaurants even accept Bevo Bucks. To find a list of participating merchants, visit www.utexas.edu/student/bevobucks.

BEST DATE RESTAURANTS

CLAY PIT

This restaurant's delicious cuisine and unique ambience makes it a perfect date spot for the romantic type. Try one of their house specials; it'll blow you away.

1601 Guadalupe St.

Phone: (512) 322-5131

Hours: Monday–Thursday, 11:00 a.m. – 2:00 p.m. &
5:00 p.m. – 10:00 p.m.
Friday, 11:00 a.m. – 2:00 p.m. &
5:00 p.m. – 11:00 p.m.
Saturday, 12:00 p.m. – 3:00 p.m. &
5:00 p.m. – 11:00 p.m.
Sunday, 5:00 p.m. – 10:00 p.m.

TRUDYS

This Tex-Mex fav is great for casual first daters, especially blind daters. Order the fajitas; it's a winner.

409 W. 30th St.

Phone: (512) 477-5720

Hours: Monday–Friday, 7:00 a.m. – 2:00 a.m.
Saturday–Sunday, 8:00 a.m. – 2:00 a.m.

MELLOW MUSHROOM

This ia a kooky and fun dining experience with a setting that is just as unusual as the pizzas they serve.

2426 Guadalupe St.

Phone: (512) 472-6356

Hours: Monday–Saturday, 11:00 a.m. – Business Decline
Sunday, 11:00 a.m. – Business Decline

BEST LATE-NIGHT EATS

WANFU

Despite the fact that this restaurant is off campus, it remains one of the most popular late-night eateries. This Chinese restaurant is open until four o'clock in the morning, and most students will tell you that the night chefs are much better than the lunch chefs.

    2400 E. Oltorf St.
    Phone: (512) 462-3535
    Hours: Weekdays, 11:00 a.m. - 4:00 a.m.
             Weekends, 12:00 p.m. - 4:00 a.m.

TACO CABANA

This restaurant is way better than Taco Bell and offers amazing food at reasonable prices.

    517 W. Martin Luther King Jr. Blvd.
    Phone: (512) 478-0875
    Open 24 hours

THE UNION

The Texas Student Union has something for everyone. Wendy's, Taco Bell, Chick-fil-A, and Quiznos are just a few that stay open long enough for everyone's late-night meal.

    2247 Guadalupe St.
    Hours vary

"I love how late Wanfu stays open! There's nothing like hot Chinese food at midnight!"

— DREW, Junior

BEST COFFEE

SPIDERHOUSE

The Spiderhouse is a casual dining restaurant open late. They've got a great coffee menu and an interesting vibe.

> 2908 Fruth St.
> Phone: (512) 480-9562
> Hours: Daily, 7:00 a.m. - 2:00 a.m.

METRO

Despite uncomfortable chairs (unless you are lucky enough to snag one of the couches), Metro is conveniently located next to the Co-Op and is a very independent establishment. All students should go at least once.

> 2222 Guadalupe St.
> Phone: (512) 474-5730
> Open 24 hours

STARBUCKS

If you like the chain coffeehouses, Starbucks is a good choice. They've got bakery goods, various hot and cold coffees, and tea drinks.

> 504 W. 24th St.
> Phone: (512) 472-5211
> Hours: Monday–Friday, 6:00 a.m. - 9:00 p.m.
> Saturday–Sunday, 6:30 a.m. - 9:00 p.m.

WHERE TO EAT

BEST PLACES TO TAKE YOUR PARENTS

MANGIA'S PIZZA

This is a truly unique mom and pop experience. They've got deep-dish, stuffed, and thin-crust pizzas as well as sandwiches and salads. Order one of their tasty pizzas for your parents.

3500 Guadalupe St.

Phone: (512) 302-5200

Hours: Sunday–Thursday, 10:00 a.m. – 10:00 p.m.
Friday–Saturday, 10:00 a.m. – 11:00 p.m.

COCO'S CAFÉ

It looks shady on the outside, but inside Coco's offers some of the tastiest Vietnamese food around.

1910 Guadalupe St.

Phone: (512) 236-9398

Hours: Daily, 11:00 a.m. – 10:00 p.m.

SERRANO'S

Assuming your parents can drive you off campus, or if they are into long walks, this Mexican restaurant is a must-visit. Any one of their pollo platters will hit the spot!

205 E. Longspur Blvd.

Phone: (512) 585-8559

Hours: Sunday–Thursday, 11:00 a.m. – 10:00 p.m.
Friday–Saturday, 11:00 a.m. – 11:00 p.m.

"I had never had Vietnamese food until I ate at Coco's. Now I can't get enough of it!"

– SARAH, Sophomore

PLACES TO SEE AND BE SEEN

ALAMO DRAFTHOUSE

Nationally recognized as the best movie theatre chain in the country, this fusion of full-service restaurant / movie theatre is just plain awesome. Enjoy a movie and some good food.

1120 S. Lamar Blvd.
Phone: (512) 476-1320
Hours fluctuate based on movie times

CANVAS

Canvas is a downtown spot that's a mix between an art gallery and a dance club. It's a different experience every time you go.

105 E. 5th St.
Phone: (512) 391-9181
Hours vary

WHERE TO EAT

"Alamo is by far one of the best places to hang out. My friends and I like to come here because where else can you watch a movie and enjoy great food? Popcorn doesn't count!"

– FRANK, Junior

CHEAPEST EATS

TACO SHACK
The building does look like a shack, but the food tastes gourmet.
Plus, it's cheaper than most fast food joints. Come here for some
quality tacos.

> 2825 Guadalupe St.
> Phone: (512) 320-8889
> Hours: Weekdays, 6:30 a.m. – 2:30 p.m.
>   Saturday, 7:00 a.m. – 1:00 p.m.

CHIPOTLE
This place is not the cheapest, but it's definitely the cheapest for the
amount of food you receive. Six dollars will get you a burrito the size
of a brick.

> 2230 Guadalupe St.
> Phone: (512) 320-0238
> Hours: Daily, 11:00 a.m. – 10:00 p.m.

MCDONALD'S
Located at the end of The Drag, dorm residents can raid the dollar
menu at any hour of the day.

> 414 W. Martin Luther King Jr. Blvd.
> Phone: (512) 494-0043
> Open 24 hours

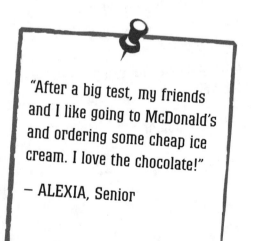

"After a big test, my friends and I like going to McDonald's and ordering some cheap ice cream. I love the chocolate!"

– ALEXIA, Senior

BEST BREAKFAST/BRUNCH

KERBEY LANE CAFE

Kerbey is an eclectic restaurant that offers a little bit of everything. From quesadillas to pumpkin pancakes, this restaurant's menu is popular with students.

2606 Guadalupe St.
Phone: (512) 477-5717
Open 24 hours

STARSEEDS

Similar to Kerbey Lane, but it's crazier. The crowd will be less campusy, but the food is great after a long night.

3101 N. I-35
Phone: (512) 478-7107
Open 24 hours

HYDE PARK BAR AND GRILL

If you want a ridiculously good breakfast, head over to this dressy restaurant. They have incredible eggs. Beware: It's not cheap!

4206 Duval St.
Phone: (512) 458-316
Hours: Daily, 11:00 a.m. – 12:00 a.m.

⊙ BEST PIZZA

MANGIA'S PIZZA

Even if your parents aren't visiting, this comic-themed pizza shop is way better than delivery and deserves your attention.

> 3500 Guadalupe St.
> Phone: (512) 302-5200
> Hours: Sunday–Thursday, 10:00 a.m. – 10:00 p.m.
>   Friday–Saturday, 10:00 a.m. – 11:00 p.m.

AUSTIN'S PIZZA

The pizza here is so delicious that the Austin Chronicle Restaurant Poll 2007 gave it the "Best Pizza" award. Try the Mopac; it's the best seller, and you'll understand why when you taste it.

> 2324 Guadalupe St.
> Phone: (512) 795-8888
> Hours: Daily, 9:00 a.m. – 12:00 a.m.

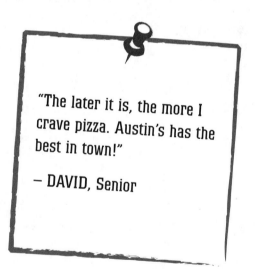

"The later it is, the more I crave pizza. Austin's has the best in town!"

– DAVID, Senior

SLICES AND ICES

Slices and Ices may be a tiny restaurant on The Drag that you overlook the first time, but come in and have some of their New York-style pizza slices and you'll be running back! And don't forget to try their frozen drinks—they are full of flavor and super refreshing.

2530 Guadalupe St.
Phone: (512) 322-9499
Call for hours

WHERE TO EAT

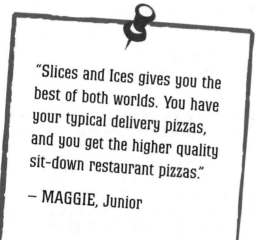

"Slices and Ices gives you the best of both worlds. You have your typical delivery pizzas, and you get the higher quality sit-down restaurant pizzas."

– MAGGIE, Junior

BEST BURGERS

DIRTY MARTINS

Their burgers are certainly not good for
you, but they are definitely good to your
taste buds. It's a little on the pricy side
but worth every penny.

    2808 Guadalupe St.

    Phone: (512) 477-3173

    Hours: Daily, 11:00 a.m. - 11:00 p.m.

BURGER TEX

This is one of the greatest burger joints in Texas. You can't live in
Austin and not go here! And they actually slice the meat before
making the patty. No other place does that. This is an essential for
all students.

    2912 Guadalupe St.

    Phone: (512) 477-8433

    Hours: Monday–Saturday, 11:00 a.m. - 9:00 p.m.

PLAYERS

Located right next to the Dobie Dormitory/Mall on campus, this
burger joint is carried by its location, affordable prices, and
oversized cooked-when-you-get-there burgers.

    300 W. Martin Luther King Jr. Blvd.

    Phone: (512) 478-929

    Hours: Monday, 12:00 a.m. - 3:00 a.m.

              Tuesday–Thursday, 10:45 a.m. - 3:00 a.m.

              Friday–Saturday, 10:45 a.m. - 3:30 a.m.

              Sunday, 10:45 a.m. - 12:00 a.m.

BEST ASIAN

MADAM MAMS

If you love Thai food, go here. They've got delicious food at reasonable prices. Try the Pad Thai with chicken. It's tender and full of flavor.

2514 Guadalupe St.
Phone: (512) 472-8306
Hours: Daily, 11:00 a.m. - 9:30 p.m.

SUNHING

Sunhing is on The Drag and has the best Mongolian Beef. Plus, they deliver, and their lunch prices are perfect for the college budget.

2801 Guadalupe St.
Phone: (512) 478-6504
Call for hours

MAGIK WOK

Magik Wok has the cheapest Chinese food around campus, and they also deliver. Delicious and affordable; what more could you ask for?

2716 Guadalupe St.
Phone: (512) 474-7770
Hours: Monday–Saturday, 11:00 a.m. - 2:30 p.m. &
4:30 p.m. - 2:00 a.m.
Sunday, 4:30 p.m. - 2:00 a.m.

"You've gotta try the veggie lo mein! It's so yummy!"

– MAUREEN, Junior

BEST MEXICAN

PAPPASITO'S

Home to possibly the best enchiladas ever created, this giant room of a restaurant has it all, including servers who make fresh guacamole while you watch.

> 6513 N. I-35
> Phone: (512) 973-0606
> Hours: Daily, 11:00 a.m. - 11:00 p.m.

TRUDY'S

Not just good for a date, Trudy's Stuffed Avocado will take your breath away and then give it back, so you can eat more.

> 409 W. 30th St.
> Phone: (512) 477-5720
> Hours: Monday-Friday, 7:00 a.m. - 2:00 a.m.
> Saturday-Sunday, 8:00 a.m. - 2:00 a.m.

TACO CABANA

It might not be real Mexican food, but it's a staple of every student's diet—a fact that probably makes nutritionists cry.

> 517 W. Martin Luther King Jr. Blvd.
> Phone: (512) 478-0875
> Open 24 hours

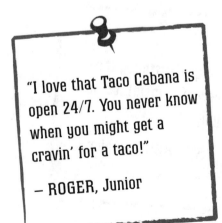

"I love that Taco Cabana is open 24/7. You never know when you might get a cravin' for a taco!"

– ROGER, Junior

BEST PLACES TO MEET PEOPLE

CAIN AND ABELS

If you want to meet the Greeks, this is where you go. This restaurant has various appetizers, burgers, and entrées. It's a fun place for hanging out with the sorority and fraternity crowd.

    2313 Rio Grande St.

    Phone: (512) 476-3201

    Hours: Monday, 12:00 a.m. – 2:00 a.m. &
                     3:00 p.m. – 2:00 a.m.
             Tuesday–Wednesday, 3:00 p.m. – 2:00 a.m.
             Thursday–Saturday, 12:00 p.m. – 2:00 a.m.
             Sunday, 12:00 p.m. – 12:00 a.m.

EXODUS

Exodus is a dance club downtown for people eighteen and up. Everyone goes here. And "everyone" is a pretty big group of people to draw from.

    302–304 E .Sixth

    Phone: (512) 477-7523

    Hours: Daily, 9:00 p.m. – 3:00 a.m.

SPIROS

Spiros is another eighteen-and-up club that has been voted one of Austin's best nightclubs for several years.

    611 Red River St.

    Phone: (512) 472-4272

    Hours: Thursday–Saturday, 10:00 p.m. – 3:00 a.m.

"Exodus is a lot of fun! No one cares if you're not a good dancer, which is great because I'm really bad at it."

– HALLIE, Senior

BEST FOOD DELIVERED TO THE DORM

TIFF'S TREATS

What could be better than hot chocolate chip cookies delivered to your dorm room? Tiff's Treats can be the answer to any problem. They will deliver snickerdoodles, sugar cookies, white chocolate macadamia nut cookies, and even brownie sundaes to your cramped dorm.

    1806 Nueces St.

    Phone: (512) 473-2600

    Hours: Monday–Friday, 10:00 a.m. - 11:45 p.m.

             Saturday–Sunday, 1:00 p.m. - 11:45 p.m.

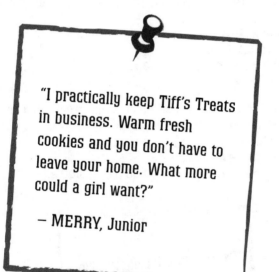

"I practically keep Tiff's Treats in business. Warm fresh cookies and you don't have to leave your home. What more could a girl want?"

– MERRY, Junior

JIMMY JOHN'S

Jimmy John's delivers high-quality sub sandwiches to your door, even in the middle of the night. It's open late and delivers some phenomenal food.

601 W. Martin Luther King Jr.
Phone: (512) 478-3111
Hours: Monday–Sunday, 11:00 a.m. - 3:00 a.m.

DOMINO'S

Students can't seem to get away from that 5-5-5 deal. If you want some pizza and you want it cheap, then Domino's is the place for you.

1900 Guadalupe St.
Phone: (512) 257-7777
Hours: Sunday–Thursday, 11:00 a.m. - 1:00 a.m.
　　　　Friday–Saturday, 11:00 a.m. - 2:00 a.m.

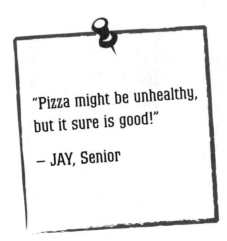

"Pizza might be unhealthy, but it sure is good!"

— JAY, Senior

⦿ BEST LOCAL FARE

HALCYON

This place is very Austin and very fun. Customers can cook their own s'mores, play board games, and of course drink coffee. There's also a tobacco shop inside.

218 W. 4th St.

Phone: (512) 472-9637

Hours: Monday-Wednesday, 7:00 a.m. - 1:00 a.m.
Thursday, 7:00 a.m. - 2:00 a.m.
Friday, 7:00 a.m. - 3:00 a.m.
Saturday, 8:00 a.m. - 3:00 a.m.
Sunday, 8:00 a.m. - 2:00 a.m.

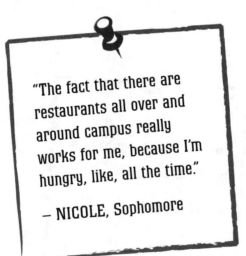

"The fact that there are restaurants all over and around campus really works for me, because I'm hungry, like, all the time."

– NICOLE, Sophomore

RUBY'S

Ruby's is a very townsy and delicious BBQ joint that offers more side options than just the typical coleslaw and baked beans. They also offer vegetarian options.

512 W. 29th St.
Phone: (512) 477-1651
Hours: Daily, 11:00 a.m. - 12:00 a.m.

HUDSON'S-ON-THE-BEND

This is a great restaurant with some pretty adventurous food. Very well-known around these parts, but pricy.

3509 Ranch Road 620 N.
Phone: (512) 266-1369
Hours: Sunday–Monday, 6:00 p.m. - 9:00 p.m.
       Tuesday–Thursday, 6:00 p.m. - 10:00 p.m.
       Friday–Saturday, 5:30 p.m. - 10:00 p.m.

WHERE TO EAT

"You really need to find a place that shows how unique Austin is, but doesn't scare your parents."

– JILL, 2007 Graduate

VEGGIE HEAVEN

This is UT's best and only vegetarian restaurant. Veggie Heaven isn't just for veggie lovers; it's for anyone who loves food. Do not be discouraged by the vegetarian menu; there is something for everyone.

1914 Guadalupe St. #A

Phone: (512) 457-1013

Hours: Weekdays, 11:00 a.m. - 8:30 p.m.
Weekends, 12:00 p.m. - 8:30 p.m.

AMY'S ICE CREAM

Amy's Ice Cream is strictly an Austin venue. It has different and delicious flavors like Brandy Biscotti and Cantaloupe. This ice-cream shop is tied to Austin and loved by all of UT's students. Plus, who doesn't want to try Guinness ice cream?

3500 Guadalupe St.

Phone: (512) 458-6895

Hours: Sunday–Thursday, 11:30 a.m. - 12:00 midnight
Friday–Saturday, 11:30 a.m. - 1:00 a.m.

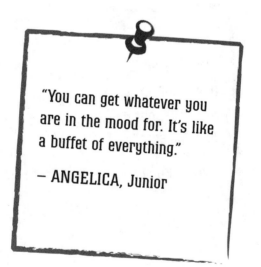

"You can get whatever you are in the mood for. It's like a buffet of everything."

– ANGELICA, Junior

◉ NOTES

_____

_____

_____

_____

_____

_____

_____

_____

_____

_____

_____

_____

_____

_____

_____

_____

_____

NUMBERS TO HAVE ON SPEED DIAL

Tiff's Treats: **(512) 473-2600**

Jimmy John's: **(512) 478-3111**

Slices and Ices: **(512) 322-9499**

Domino's: **(512) 257-7777**

⑥ RECREATION,
ENTERTAINMENT, & THE ARTS

The best part about any college guide is that students can read about all the cool stuff their new city has to offer. Austin has everything you could possibly need and way too much more. You can swim, watch bats fly out at dusk, go to a park or natural spring, go ice skating, see movies, and hear tons of live music. What more could you want? Oh, and the best part is that Austin is not like the smaller cities that surround it. Everything stays open until at least midnight or later. You can have fun, and you can have it at any time of the day . . . or night.

LIVE MUSIC VENUES

Austin is famous for its music scene, often called the "live music capital of the world." No matter what you are looking for, mosh pits and angry screams, smooth jazz and smoky rooms, pop songs and acoustic guitars, or emo bands with boys who wear eye liner, you can find it at any of the live music venues in Austin.

CACTUS CAFÉ

Located inside the Texas Union, Cactus Café is the place to hear some great acoustic music. It hosts some smaller bands and singer/songwriters as well as bigger acts like the Dixie Chicks, Ani DiFranco, Lyle Lovett, and Alison Krauss. This cozy joint is truly a gem when it comes to on-campus musical entertainment.

> 2247 Guadalupe St
> Austin, TX 78705
> **Phone:** (512) 475-6515

ELEPHANT ROOM

This is a fun jazz club that looks like it's straight from a Hollywood set. It has a below street-level funk factor, and it features both local and national acts. It's free most weeknights. There's a small cover charge on the weekends.

> 315 Congress Ave.
> Austin, TX 78701
> **Phone:** (512) 473-2279

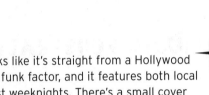

"The Elephant Room is really cool and showcases some very talented jazz musicians."

– AMY, Junior

BROKEN SPOKE

If you love honky-tonk music and enjoy hearing local musicians sing, then check out Broken Spoke. It's an old-fashioned dance hall where you and your friends can dance to live country music.

3201 S. Lamar Blvd.
Austin, TX 78704
Phone: (512) 442-6189

LA ZONA ROSA

La Zona Rosa is a live-music venue that hosts a variety of local and national acts such as Joss Stone, Patti Smith, and Gavin DeGraw. All music genres are performed here, including rock, Latin, blues, and jazz music.

612 W. 4th St.
Austin, TX 78701
Phone: (512) 263-4146

⦿ MUSIC FESTIVALS IN AUSTIN

You can also hear live music at the various Austin music festivals. The most famous of these are **Austin City Limits (ACL)** and **South by SouthWest (SXSW)**.

AUSTIN CITY LIMITS MUSIC FESTIVAL

The **Austin City Limits** music festival (don't confuse it with the TV show) is a three-day art and music festival that's held every year at Zilker Park. Thousands of out-of-towners flock to Austin for a few days of live music from more than 130 bands on eight stages. Genres include rock, country, folk, indie, Americana, hip hop, and more. More than sixty-five thousand people come to this festival. This is definitely the place to be when it comes to experiencing the music you love. In the past, performers have included Bob Dylan, Bjork, the Killers, Ryan Adams, and Los Lonely Boys.

AUSTIN CITY LIMITS AT ZILKER PARK

2100 Barton Springs Rd.
Austin, TX 78746
www.aclfestival.com

SOUTH BY SOUTHWEST (SXSW) FESTIVAL

This music festival is one of the largest in the United States. It takes place every year downtown at the Austin Convention Center. Hundreds of musical performers from all over the world perform on more than fifty stages. This festival is truly exciting. At the 2007 SXSW Festival, there were over 1,400 acts from every style of music imaginable, from pop and country to electronica.

SOUTH BY SOUTH WEST FESTIVAL
AT THE AUSTIN CONVENTION CENTER

500 East Cesar Chavez St.
Austin, TX 78701
Phone: (512) 404-4000
www.sxsw.com

RECREATION
ENTERTAINMENT

"You can't miss the South by Southwest Festival. They have some of the best bands! It's so much fun."

– LILLY, Junior

CAMPUS RECREATION CENTER

UNIVERSITY OF TEXAS RECREATION CENTER

Located right next to the football stadium and Gregory Gym, the UT Rec Center has everything to suit your needs. There are basketball courts, volleyball courts, weight rooms, two international-size squash courts, an exercise lounge, aerobic and dance rooms, and several multipurpose rooms. Overall, it is 120,000 square feet!

Located south of the Moncrief-Neuhaus Athletic Center
www.utrecsports.org

UT Informal Recreation: (512) 471-6370
UT Outdoor Recreation: (512) 471-8047
      Hours: Monday–Thursday, 6:00 a.m. – 11:00 p.m.
              Friday, 6:00 a.m. – 8:00 p.m.
              Saturday, 8:00 a.m. – 8:00 p.m.
              Sunday, 10:00 a.m. – 11:00 p.m.

"The UT Rec Center is a great place to go relieve some stress before a big exam!"

– ARI, Junior

PARKS

After a long and stressful week of classes, you can always find UT students relaxing and hanging out with their friends at local parks.

ZILKER METROPOLITAN PARK
One of the most popular outside attractions in Austin, this park has everything from a swimming pool to its botanical gardens. Spanning more than three hundred acres, this park will amaze you every time you go.

2100 Barton Springs Rd.
Austin, TX 78746

BARTON SPRINGS
On a hot day, this natural swimming hole is crawling with students taking a refreshing swim. The pool is fed from underground springs and is open year-round.

2101 Barton Springs Rd.
Austin, TX 78704
Phone: (512) 476-9044

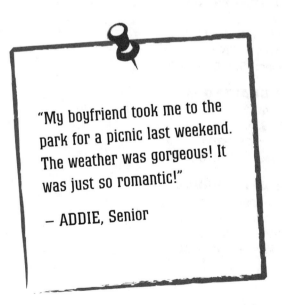

"My boyfriend took me to the park for a picnic last weekend. The weather was gorgeous! It was just so romantic!"

– ADDIE, Senior

● CINEMAS

If you're in the mood to catch a new release, you have many choices here. Austin is home to a variety of regular and nontraditional movie theatres.

ALAMO DRAFTHOUSE

The Alamo Drafthouse movie theater chain is an authentic Texas experience you shouldn't miss. There are four Alamo Drafthouse locations in Austin: Lake Creek, South Lamar, the Village Shopping Center, and downtown. Most of these are restaurant/movie theater combinations that play new releases. The downtown venue is unique. Rather than playing the usual new movie releases, this venue hosts air guitar competitions, '90s boy band sing-a-longs, and *Rocky Horror Picture Show* viewings every week.

You should dress up for the *Rocky Horror Picture Show* viewings. If you don't, they'll know it's your first time and you will have to get up in front of everyone and sing.

ALAMO DRAFTHOUSE
(Lake Creek)
> 13729 Research Blvd.
> Austin, TX 78750
> **Phone: (512) 219-7800**

ALAMO DRAFTHOUSE
(South Lamar)
> 1120 South Lamar
> Austin, TX 78704
> **Phone: (512) 476-1320**

ALAMO DRAFTHOUSE
(Village Shopping Center)
> 2700 W. Anderson Ln.
> Austin, TX 78757
> **Phone: (512) 476-1320**

ALAMO DRAFTHOUSE
(Downtown)
>409 Colorado St. #B
>Austin, TX 78701
>**Phone: (512) 476-1320**

DOBIE MALL THEATER
This little art house movie theater is located on campus. Although it doesn't play mainstream movies, you will always see something different and edgy here. Most of the movies here are independent films.
>2021 Guadalupe St.
>Austin, TX 78705
>**Phone: (512) 472-3456**

REGAL CINEMAS METROPOLITAN 14
This is a regular movie theater that plays new releases. They also offer student discounts.
>901 Little Texas Ln.
>Austin, TX 78745
>**Phone: (512) 447-0101**

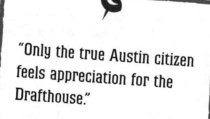

"Only the true Austin citizen feels appreciation for the Drafthouse."

– BROOKE, Graduate

THEATERS

Watching a theater show in Austin is a unique experience. Many theaters in town enjoy straying from the norm and inventing new ways to entertain the audience.

ESTHER'S FOLLIES

This comedy troupe puts on a show every weekend that pokes fun at everything. It's hilarious and a must-see! Tickets are typically between $18 and $23. Students get a $2 discount.

525 E. 6th St.
Austin, TX 78701
Phone: (512) 320-0553

ZACHARY SCOTT THEATER CENTER

This established performance center is always looking for ways to reinvent their shows, and it's always great to see them do it. In 2007, they performed a bilingual version of *Jesus Christ, Superstar*. A truly strange and entertaining show for the audience!

1510 Toomey Rd.
Austin, TX 78704
Phone: **(512) 476-0541**
(512) 476-0594

UT THEATER

If you have trouble getting off campus to see the city theater scene, then go see a University of Texas production. It only costs $10 for students, and they put on an entertaining show. To get tickets, drop by the UTPAC Box Office in Bass Concert Hall.

UTPAC Box Office
Bass Concert Hall
23rd and Robert Dedman Dr.
Austin, TX 78712
Phone: (512) 471-4444

MUSEUMS

There are a few museums on campus students can explore. The **Harry Ransom Center** and the newly built **Blanton Museum** are two museums on campus that house a variety of interesting exhibits. You can also find museums in Austin.

THE HARRY RANSOM CENTER

Though it can be argued that this museum is part library, it houses some of the best historical documents of this century, like the original notes that Carl Bernstein and Bob Woodward took when they were investigating the Watergate scandal. There's a lot of impressive stuff here.

> 300 West 21st St.
> Austin, TX 78712
> **Phone: (512) 471-8944**

THE BLANTON MUSEUM OF ART

The Blanton is home to some of the most conceptually intriguing exhibits to ever hit a university museum. Art history classes have labs in this museum. It's the newest university-owned museum.

> 200 East Martin Luther King Jr.
> Austin, TX 78701
> **Phone: (512) 471-5482**

AUSTIN MUSEUM OF ART

This museum has a collection of twentieth-century art, including paintings, drawings, photographs, and even sculptures. If you're interested in art, take a peek inside this place.

> 823 Congress Ave. #100
> Austin, TX 78701
> **Phone: (512) 495-9224**

O. HENRY HOME AND MUSEUM

If you're a fan of the writer William Sydney Porter, you should visit this place. What used to be his home has now been turned into a museum full of artifacts and memorabilia from his life.

> 409 East Fifth St.
> Austin, TX 78701
> **Phone: (512) 472-1903**

RECREATION
ENTERTAINMENT

BOWLING ALLEYS

The only place to go bowling on campus is the **Texas Underground**. Located in the basement of the Texas Union, this place has an arcade, billiard tables, and a big-screen TV that bowlers can watch in between turns. You can also find bowling alleys off campus.

> 2247 Guadalupe St.
> Austin, TX 78712
> **Phone: (512) 475-6670**

HIGHLAND LANES

> 8909 Burnet Rd.
> Austin, TX 78757
> **Phone: (512) 458-1215**

WESTGATE LANES

> 2701 W. William Cannon
> Austin, TX 78745
> **Phone: (512) 441-2695**

AMF SHOWPLACE LANES

> 9504 N. I-35
> Austin, TX 78753
> **Phone: (512) 834-7733**

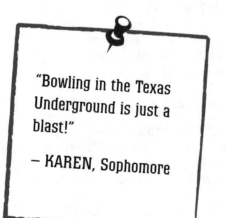

"Bowling in the Texas Underground is just a blast!"

– KAREN, Sophomore

ICE SKATING AND ROLLER SKATING

When it gets hot and you want to cool off, grab a couple of your friends and go ice skating at the Chaparral Ice Center inside the Northcross Mall. If you don't have any skates, rent a pair from them! They also offer skating classes for all skill levels.

CHAPARRAL ICE CENTER
Northcross Mall
2525 West Anderson Ln.
Austin, TX 78728
Phone: (512) 451-5102

If you're interested in roller skating, then head over to the **Playland Skate Center**. They have an extra-large rink with some pretty cool lights. Admission is usually between $5 and $7, depending on what day you go.

PLAYLAND SKATE CENTER
8822 McCann Dr.
Austin, TX 78757
Phone: (512) 452-1901

GYMS

If you're in the mood to work out, head over to the Gregory Gym. It is free for UT students and has a state-of-the-art facility, including multiple pools, racquet ball courts, ping-pong tables, elliptical machines, a rock-climbing wall, and an overwhelming number of weights.

GREGORY GYMNASIUM
2101 Speedway
Austin, TX 78712
Phone: (512) 471-6370

If for some reason you want to find a gym off campus, then just drive to the nearby **24 Hour Fitness**, open (you guessed it) for twenty-four hours a day. It's only a five-minute drive from campus.

24 HOUR FITNESS
10616 Research Blvd.
Austin, TX 78759
Phone: (512) 794-9151

DAY TRIPS

SOUTH PADRE ISLAND

One of the most popular beach spots for the entire student body, South Padre is a nice and relaxing place to go. Located next to the Gulf of Mexico, this place has miles of beautiful beaches and is the best place to go fishing in Texas. It's extremely fun, considering most of the people you meet there also go to UT.

7355 Padre Blvd.
South Padre Island, TX 78597
Phone: (800) SOPADRE

SCHLITTERBAHN

Only about an hour away from campus, this water park is the perfect spot for a day trip. It's one of the most elaborate water parks in the country and so big that it would take you an entire day to experience the whole thing. Before you leave, you need to try the Hillside Tube Chute; it's awesome!

381 East Austin St.
New Braunfels, TX 78130
Phone: (830) 625-2351

TUBING IN NEW BRAUNFELS

Taking a day trip (or weekend getaway) to New Braunfels doesn't have to end at the Schlitterbahn water resort. For a relaxing day in the sun, simply rent a bunch of inner tubes and float down the river. You can rent tubes at **Texas Tubes** for a fee.

TexasTubes.com
250 Meusebach Dr.
New Braunfels, TX 78130
Phone: (830) 626-9900

◉ NOTES

RECREATION
ENTERTAINMENT

NUMBERS TO HAVE ON SPEED DIAL

UT Informal Recreation: **(512) 471-6370**

UT Outdoor Recreation: **(512) 471-8047**

⑦ STOP N SHOP

No college town can really be perfect without a great venue for shopping, and Austin doesn't fail to deliver. Whether you are into independent boutiques or large chains, cheaper vintage or pricy labels, emo shirts or classic sports attire, this city has it all. Some of these stores are even within walking distance from campus. You can find grocery stores, décor for your room, discount stores, and even trendy clothing boutiques on the Drag. If you can't find what you're looking for here, then head over to the nearby malls. There are city buses that will take you to and from the mall. Shopping has never been easier!

GROCERY STORES

There are a number of grocery stores in Austin, but the H-E-B is the most popular place.

H-E-B

If you go to school in Austin, chances are you will go to H-E-B. This massive grocery store chain has its own pharmacy as well as the regular groceries. But the reason students love H-E-B so much? It's cheap, and they always have great coupons. Unfortunately it's off campus, so you'll need to get a ride.

4001 N. Lamar Blvd.
Phone: (512) 458-3068

WHEATSVILLE CO-OP

Located on the Drag, the Wheatsville Co-Op offers more organic and natural options for food. Vegans and vegetarians, this is the perfect place for you. They offer a nice selection of locally produced food and organic, pesticide-free veggies. They even sell organic smoothies and sodas.

3101 Guadalupe St.
Phone: (512) 478-2667

SPEEDWAY GROCERY

If you're looking to browse a smaller grocery store, then this is it. They offer a nice selection.

3707 Speedway
Phone: (512) 472-8850

⦿ PHARMACIES

CVS
Located on The Drag, this drug store is one of the closest places to pick up that over-the-counter medication.
> 2927 Guadalupe St.
> **Phone: (512) 474-2323**

NAU PHARMACY
This place is another option, but it's more expensive and farther away from campus.
> 2406 San Gabriel St.
> **Phone: (512) 472-1424**

⦿ DISCOUNT STORES

BLUE VELVET
Located near campus, on 21st and Guadalupe, this is your classic thrift store. It is very indie and cheap. It's unlikely you'll find brand names at this place.
> 2100 Guadalupe St. #B
> **Phone: (512) 472-9399**

BUFFALO EXCHANGE
You can find some very good deals on nice clothes at the Buffalo Exchange. This thrift store sells some brand names, like Abercrombie and American Eagle, and is located on The Drag.
> 2904 Guadalupe St.
> **Phone: (512) 480-9922**

TOP DRAWER THRIFT SHOP
If you want to help others while finding some real treasure for cheap, come to Top Drawer Thrift Shop. The proceeds made at the shop go to Project Transitions, which provides support to those living with HIV and AIDS.
> 4902 Burnet Rd.
> **Phone: (512) 454-5161**

DÉCOR FOR THE DORM

URBAN OUTFITTERS

Located right on The Drag, this weird store has attitude, funk, and youth. It's certain that you'll find a lamp, rug, or strange chair that you'll want to snatch up.

2406 Guadalupe St.
Phone: (512) 472-1621

IKEA

Filled with cheap yet classy buys, this store is almost too big. IKEA has some room models that are specifically designed for the square footage of a dorm. This is an excellent source for conserving space while still looking chic.

4000 N. I H 35
Round Rock, TX 78681
Phone: (512) 828-4532

STOP N
SHOP

"IKEA isn't just a place you go to get one thing. IKEA is an event. And it's perfect for college living."

– AVA, Sophomore

TARGET

Target is another option for dorm décor. They sell some fun furniture marketed toward college students. Their prices are pretty reasonable for some of the smaller items.

2300 W. Ben White Blvd.
Phone: (512) 445-2266

BEST BUY

Come here to buy the latest CD players, digital cameras, and movies. This is your entertainment headquarters.

9607 Research Blvd.
Phone: (512) 795-0014

WAL-MART SUPERCENTER

They carry a lot of useful items, and their low prices are bound to fit any college student's budget.

710 E. Ben White Blvd.
Phone: (512) 443-6601

BED, BATH & BEYOND

This place can be pricey, but they have a wide selection of quality merchandise.

5400 Brodie Ln #300
Sunset Valley, TX 78745
Phone: (512) 892-7110

MALLS AND SHOPPING CENTERS

Both the **Highland Mall** and the **Barton Creek Mall** have bus routes on city buses that will take you from campus of the mall and back. It's very convenient if you don't have a car.

HIGHLAND MALL

This mall is the closest to campus, and it's also the smallest. It doesn't have the size or selection of the other malls, but you can still find a few good deals here.

6001 Airport Blvd.
Phone: (512) 454-9656

BARTON CREEK MALL

Although it's farther away from campus, this mall is more comprehensive and home to the only Apple store in the area. It also has two movie theaters and various brand-name stores like Express, Aeropostale, and Abercrombie and Fitch.

2901 S. Capital of Texas Hwy.
Phone: (512) 327-7041

ARBORETUM

This mall has a limited selection of stores but is home to a few brand names, including Banana Republic, Express, Gap, Victoria's Secret, and Nine West.

9607 Research Blvd.
Phone: (512) 338-4437

"Whether I want to spend a lot of money or a little money, I can always find something new to wear on The Drag."

– RYAN, Junior

GATEWAY SHOPPING CENTERS

If you're looking for some dorm décor, Gateway has several stores dedicated to selling rugs, furniture, and other accessories. It also has a movie theater and several restaurants.

9607 Research Blvd.
Phone: (512) 338-4755

PRIME OUTLETS AT SAN MARCOS

Although it's not located in Austin, this place has over 130 brand name stores, including Neiman Marcus, Coach, BeBe, and Off 5th Saks Fifth Avenue Outlet. It's also a really pretty mall, designed after the Piazza San Marco in Venice, Italy.

3939 S. I-35 #300
San Marcos, TX 78666
Phone: (512) 396-2200

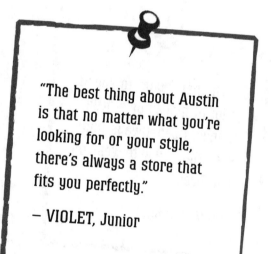

"The best thing about Austin is that no matter what you're looking for or your style, there's always a store that fits you perfectly."

– VIOLET, Junior

MEN'S AND WOMEN'S CLOTHING

DIESEL

This high-end trendy store is conveniently located on The Drag and offers quality clothing but at a price. After all, brand names never come cheap. It's entirely possible to drop $200 on a pair of designer jeans.

2120 Guadalupe St.
Phone: (512) 478-2555

BY GEORGE

If you love boutiques, this is the store for you. It is a boutique in every sense of the word. It's pricey, but the clothes are very trendy and hip.

524 N. Lamar Blvd.
Phone: (512) 472-5951

NEIMAN MARCUS

This world-famous store is super expensive, but their clothes, handbags, and accessories are very stylish. They sell a lot of famous designer clothing like Prada and Vera Wang.

4115 S. Capital of Texas Hwy.
Phone: (512) 447-0701

CREAM VINTAGE

If you're looking for some really weird, quality vintage clothing, then you'll love this place. Located on The Drag, they sell interesting accessories and vintage clothing for men and women.

2532 Guadalupe St.
Phone: (512) 474-8787

MANJU'S

You can find this place on The Drag. They sell a variety of women's clothing. They don't sell any brand names, but all their stuff is pretty edgy and unique.

2424 Guadalupe St.
Phone: (512) 474-0637

◉ MUSIC STORES

WATERLOO RECORDS

A truly authentic music shop, this record store (yes, they still sell actual records) has had the same business policies since it opened in the early '80s. You can listen to anything before you buy it, and you can return merchandise with no questions asked. They are truly interested in getting the joy of music spread throughout Austin. They even host events for up-and-coming bands. It's a must-visit!

600 N. Lamar Blvd. #A
Phone: (512) 474-2500

MUSIC MANIA

They offer a large selection of rap, soul, and R&B music. They also have great deals on vinyl.

3909 N. I-35 #D1
Phone: (512) 451-3361

◉ JEWELERS

NOMADIC NOTIONS

This place is one of the biggest bead retail stores you will find in town. You can create your own jewelry here, and they even offer classes that teach beading techniques.

3010 W. Anderson Ln. #C
Phone: (512) 454-0001

PERSONAL ADORNMENTS

This is another jewelry shop you can find on The Drag.

1705 Guadalupe St.
Phone: (512) 477-5355

CRYSTAL WORKS

This shop specializes in crystals and stones.

908 W. 12th St. #A
Phone: (512) 472-5597

GREEK APPAREL

THE CO-OP

The Co-Op has just about everything you will need before you start the year: textbooks, pens, paper, binders, and most importantly, UT clothing! No UT student is officially a Longhorn until they buy their very own UT shirt or sweatpants.

2246 Guadalupe St.
Phone: (512) 476-7211

TYLER'S SPORTING GOODS STORE

Proud seller of the "Keep Austin Weird" T-shirts, this is the place to shop for all the nonofficial UT stuff.

2338 Guadalupe St.
Phone: (512) 478-5500

STOP N SHOP

TIP

If you need to save a little money, then two doors down from the actual Co-Op is the Co-Op Outlet, which is MUCH cheaper.

⦿ SPORTING GOODS

ACADEMY SPORTS AND OUTDOORS

This is the typical sporting goods store. They sell everything from fitness and athletic equipment to hunting and camping gear.

7513 N. I-35
Phone: (512) 407-6310

REI

REI sells mostly gear, equipment, and clothing for outdoor sports. Whether you're into cycling, camping, kayaking, or skiing, you can find your essentials here.

705 N. Lamar Blvd.
Phone: (512) 320-8027

"I always go to REI to buy my camping gear. They have a nice selection of merchandise at reasonable prices."

– BARRY, Junior

⊙ BOOKSTORES

BORDERS BOOKS AND MUSIC
Borders is a place to buy all kinds of books. They have some textbooks, fiction, and nonfiction. They also sell CDs and movies.

4477 S. Lamar Blvd. #600
Phone: (512) 891-8974

BARNES & NOBLE BOOKSELLERS ARBORETUM
Like Borders, this place sells all kinds of books, CDs, and movies.

10000 Research Blvd.
Phone: (512) 418-8985

BOOK PEOPLE
Book People is an independently owned bookstore with four stories of merchandise. This is one of the few places that will carry that strange book you want that no one else has. It has pretty much everything, and you could easily spend a day reading in that place.

603 N. Lamar Blvd.
Phone: (512) 472-5050

STOP N SHOP

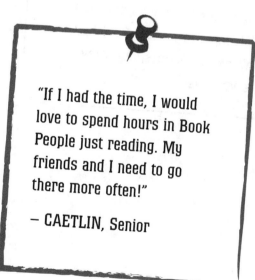

"If I had the time, I would love to spend hours in Book People just reading. My friends and I need to go there more often!"

— CAETLIN, Senior

THE CO-OP

If you need textbooks, this is where you should go. Most of the time they'll have all the books you'll need for classes, and they will buy them back for cash at the end of the year. Textbooks tend to be ridiculously expensive at the Co-Op. Convenience here comes at a hefty price.

2246 Guadalupe St.
Phone: (512) 476-7211

TIP

Of all these places, the best way to sell your textbooks back is to go straight to the Co-Op. They don't need receipts, and they'll give you cash.

● NOTES

(blank ruled lines)

NUMBERS TO HAVE ON SPEED DIAL

The Co-Op: **(512) 476-7211**

H-E-B: **(512) 458-3068**

CVS Pharmacy: **(512) 474-2323**

STOP N SHOP

⑧ BLAH, BLAH
& WHATEVER

By now you've probably learned that UT is anything but boring. The campus and the city have small idiosyncrasies that make it what it is. As you spend more time here, you'll fall in love with the little things that make Austin and UT so special. This chapter will give you a sneak peek at these quirks, from the urban legends roaming campus to campus slang. And because Austin is such an incredible city, surely you'll want to share it with your parents when they visit. Read on and you'll also find the closest hotels and churches.

LOCAL HOTELS

BEST WESTERN SEVILLE PLAZA INN
4323 S. I-35
Austin, TX 78744
Phone: (512) 447-5511

HAMPTON INN NORTH
7619 N. I-35
Austin, TX 78752
Phone: (512) 452-3300

HOLIDAY INN EXPRESS
7622 N. I-35
Austin, TX 78752
Phone: (877) 784-6835

OMNI AUSTIN HOTEL
700 San Jacinto Blvd.
Austin, TX 78701
Phone: (512) 476-3700

For more hotels, go to www.hotelsnearcampus.com.

BLAH, BLAH

LOCAL HOUSES OF WORSHIP

Whatever your religious preference is, you can find a house of worship that fits your needs. Austin offers a variety of Catholic and Christian churches, several temples and synagogues, and a few places of worship for Eastern faiths.

To find a church in Austin, look at www.churchsearch.com/austin/home.htm.

CAMPUS SLANG

The Drag: Also known as Guadalupe Street. The Drag runs parallel to the edge of campus and holds the Co-Op and more restaurants than you can think of. You seem to find something new on The Drag every time you go.

PCL: This is the nickname of the Perry-Castaneda Library.

FAC: This is another name for the Flawn Academic Center.

TXU: This is another name for the Texas Union.

SSB: This is the Student Services Building.

UTC: Also known as the University Teaching Center, this building is where the larger freshmen courses are taught.

West Mall: This is the courtyard-like area outside the Union and FAC.

WEL: This is Welch Hall, a HUGE building that you will have almost ev[ery] science class in.

The Six Pack: This is the nickname for the six buildings on campus that stand like a six pack of sodas or abdominal muscles. Three are lined up on one side of a small grassy area and the other three on the opposite side. These buildings are Parlin, Batts, Mezes, Benedict, Calhoun, and Rainey. Learn them because most liberal arts classes take place here. All of your foreign language classes will most likely be in the Six Pack.

BLAH, BLAH

"It's actually really easy to pick up the lingo and remember where everything is. As soon as you get it, you feel like you belong."

— KRISSY, Sophomore

UNIVERSITY VIOLATIONS

Like any university, one of the most inexcusable violations is plagiarism. Copying or cheating is the easiest way to get kicked out of school, and UT is pretty strict about it.

UT also has a very strict policy on illegal drug and alcohol violations. If a student is caught in possession of, using, or distributing an illegal drug, the university will, at a minimum, require a suspension of a determined time period. And further disciplinary matters will result in expulsion, fines, or probation should they be necessary. The same punishments go for underage drinking.

LOCAL LAWS

The legal BAC limit to drive in Texas is under .08. After that, a DWI (Driving While Intoxicated) will be issued. First offense requires up to $2,000 fine, from 72 hours to 180 days in jail, and license removal from 90 days to a year. As of 2001, it is illegal to possess any open container containing alcohol while driving a car. It must be stowed in the trunk or in the glove compartment.

BLAH, BLAH

"The penalties for a DWI are so severe that it's dumb to even think of getting in a car and driving drunk.

– MOLLY, Senior

⦿ DID YA KNOW?

URBAN LEGENDS

There is a long-standing urban legend that the infamous UT Tower was designed by a graduate of Rice University, one of UT's rival schools. If you look at the tower diagonally (where one of the edges is straight ahead), you can see that the clock faces make up two eyes, and the main segment of the corner of the tower makes the face of an owl (Rice University's mascot).

Jester dormitory is thought to have been designed by a prison architect. It's also rumored that Jester is so large that it has its own zip code. There's also the rumor that Jester used to be the second-largest dorm in the world, until the largest dorm in Russia burnt down, and now it's the first.

"There are so many rumors at Jester . . . and I think some of them might be true. It's so big."

— ALICE, Sophomore

RANDOM FACTS

- In a 2004 survey, the *Times of London* ranked the University of Texas at Austin the 15th best university in the world.

- The Tower is not only the most recognizable landmark in Austin; it's also six feet taller than the Texas Capitol.

- UT Austin was considered one of America's Public Ivies in the 2001 book *The Public Ivies: America's Flagship Public Institutions* by Howard and Matthew Greene.

- The public television show *Austin City Limits* is actually filmed in a studio on UT's campus.

- The official fight song, "Texas Fight," was listed as one of the ten most inspiring college fight songs in a 1990 national study.

UNIVERSITY WEB ADDRESSES

Home: www.utexas.edu

Austin Events Directory: www.utexas.edu/austin

Library: www.lib.utexas.edu

UT Direct: https://utdirect.utexas.edu/utdirect

E-mail Server: http://webmail.utexas.edu

Athletic Center: www.utexas.edu/athletics

Student Newspaper *The Daily Texan*: www.dailytexanonline.com

University Health Services: http://healthyhorns.utexas.edu

Registrar Home: www.utexas.edu/student/registrar

Information Technology Service: www.utexas.edu/its

Advising Help Page: www.utexas.edu/academic/advising

University Calendars Home Page: www.utexas.edu/calendars

BLAH, BLAH

◉ NOTES

_____

_____

_____

_____

_____

_____

_____

_____

_____

_____

_____

_____

_____

NUMBERS TO HAVE ON SPEED DIAL

UT Outdoor Recreation Office:
(512) 471-3116

Police (Emergency): **911**

ITS Help Desk: **(512) 475-9400**

WANT TO CHECK OUT WHAT OTHER CGUIDES ARE AVAILABLE?

Visit our website at
www.cguides.net

FIND OUT THE LATEST WHERE-TO-GO AND WHAT-TO-KNOW
INFORMATION FOR THE UNIVERSITY OF TEXAS
http://utexas.cguides.net

RANK THE BEST PIZZA

POST A CAMPUS EVENT

LOOK FOR COUPONS AND DEALS

CHECK OUT WHAT'S HAPPENING

AND SO MUCH MORE!